Dedicated to the witness of

Saint John Paul II,

and also to my father,
who has always supported
my artistic pursuits.

Para Tony y Marisol Angelini,

Fabiola Garza

Jn 21:17

A Boy Who Became Pope

The Story of Saint John Paul II

Written & Illustrated by
Fabiola Garza

Pauline
BOOKS & MEDIA
Boston

It was deep in the month of May. The wind whistled through the fields of a small country town in the heart of Poland. A little boy was born that day. His parents named him Karol. But everyone called him Lolek.

The seasons went quickly by, and
Lolek grew. He was the second-best goalie
in town. But one day he slipped and missed
the ball. His best friend Jerzy helped him
to his feet. "Well, you can't be great *all* the
time," he said.

Lolek disagreed. "Let's race to the lake and whoever swims to the other side first is the greatest." And off they ran.

Lolek lost the race, but he got home in time for supper.

"Lolek, be very quiet," Papa said. "Your mother is sick and needs rest."

The next day she didn't seem much better —or the next. Lolek hoped to cheer her up. So he plucked a red poppy from the field and gave it to her.

"I brought you a present," he whispered.

She thanked him with a smile.

"Lolek, soon I am going to meet God," his mother said with a tear in her eye.

"You won't be coming back, Mama, will you?"

"No, Lolek. I'm dying. But I'll always watch over you."

"Mama, I promise I'll do great things."

"I'm sure you will," she said softly. "But there is something even more important. Lolek, who do you love most?"

"I love you and Papa and Edmund and—"

"Yes, but *who* do you love the *most*?"

Lolek grew quiet. He didn't know how to answer.

"Love is the greatest gift we receive, and the greatest we can give. Someday you'll have an answer to my question. And when you know who you love most, you'll also know what to do."

He placed the poppy in a cup by the window. Then he kissed his mother goodbye. Lolek was very sad.

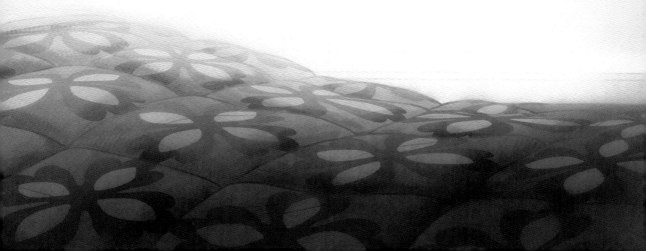

Time passed. One day, Lolek woke up to the gentle morning breeze. His broken heart felt much better. He was also proud of his older brother, Edmund. He had become a fine doctor.

On the way to church, Edmund asked, "So what do you want to be when *you* grow up?"

"Me? I want to be an actor on the stage!"

"I think that's a great dream," Edmund replied.

Lolek was glad. If Edmund thought being an actor was a good idea, then it had to be.

Edmund encouraged Lolek by inviting him to perform for his patients at the hospital. At first, Lolek was nervous. But once he began, he became calm. Acting came naturally to him.

One winter evening, the wind howled in the biting cold. Edmund told Lolek to stay home because many of his patients had caught a deadly fever. Lolek watched as his brother was swallowed by the snowstorm. He hoped Edmund would be safe. Lolek slept by the window until his father woke him up.

"Lolek, hurry, put your coat on. There's trouble at the hospital." In a blink they were on their way, but Lolek didn't know why they were in such a hurry.

When they got to the hospital, Lolek didn't see his brother anywhere. Everyone was busy. Then Lolek saw that Edmund was sick in bed. He was as pale as Mama had been before she died.

Lolek felt his face grow hot.

"Edmund, please don't die! I love you so much," he pleaded.

"I love you, too. I'll just have to love you from heaven." Edmund's voice grew weaker. "I'm going to meet God and see Mama again. Just remember Mama's question, Lolek. *Who do you love most?*"

Lolek's thoughts carried him away to warm summer memories and fields full of poppies. And then there was another goodbye. It hurt him very much.

In time, Lolek's heart mended. He smiled easily
as he sped across the square to meet Father Leonard
at Saint Mary's Church. Lolek polished the statues
and swept the floor, and when he was done, the kind
priest suggested that he pray for a bit.

Meanwhile, Jerzy sat in the noon sun waiting for his best friend. He had something very important to tell Lolek. When he was tired of waiting, Jerzy went to the church to see if his friend was there. He pulled at the heavy door. Then, all of a sudden, a lady clutched his arm. She frowned at him.

"You're not allowed in there," she clucked. "You're a Jew."

Lolek heard what she said and ran outside.

"Ma'am, my father taught me we're all God's children. Jerzy can come into the church if he wants to!" Lolek said.

Lolek took Jerzy by the hand and ran off. They left the woman with Father Leonard.

The two boys spent the day at Jerzy's house. At twilight, the stars began to fill the sky. Jerzy suddenly remembered the news he had wanted to share with his friend.

"Lolek, I forgot to tell you! We both passed our exams."

"We did? We're going to have so much fun together in high school!" Lolek exclaimed.

Jerzy shrugged. "Yeah, but you'll be too busy doing great things to have fun anymore."

"We can have fun *and* do great things. I promise."

High school was fun, but Lolek's favorite part about it was being an actor in school plays. One of his friends helped Lolek get his first big role. His performance was a great success. Applause filled the theater on opening night. Right after the curtain closed Lolek ran to thank his friend for helping him get the part. When he found her, her eyes were shiny with tears.

"What's wrong?" Lolek asked.

"Haven't you heard the rumors?" she replied.

"Yes, I heard that the Nazis are threatening Jewish people. And it won't be long before their soldiers march into Poland. They will try to do the same things here."

"Soon my family and I will have to leave so we can be safe."

The idea that anyone would hurt his Jewish friends upset him.

A few days later Lolek and Jerzy talked about
everything that was happening.

"War is coming and many of our friends are
leaving," said Lolek sadly.

"You know I will have to go too," Jerzy responded.
"It isn't safe for us to stay here."

"I know," Lolek replied. "Some of our Jewish neighbors have already escaped to other countries. Others are being watched."

"Lolek, you have always been a good friend. I will miss you," said Jerzy.

"I'll miss you too," said Lolek. His heart tightened in his chest. "I hope we'll see each other soon."

But neither really knew when—or if—they would see each other again.

Soon the war came to Poland and covered the country in darkness.

Lolek was now a young man and his world was changing quickly. His Jewish friends who hadn't left Poland were in hiding. Some had been captured. Lolek and his father moved to a tiny apartment in the city. There, Lolek could continue his studies. He often read by candlelight. After dark they could hear scuffles, shouts, and the heavy tread of soldiers. Those sounds made people afraid to go out at night.

When schools began to close and some of his teachers were arrested, Lolek went to work in a stone quarry. His fellow workers were good men. Many of them offered to work in Lolek's place when he needed to study. There wasn't enough food to eat, but he fed his mind with books.

One day a blaster at the quarry said something unexpected. "Lolek, you give us all hope. Have you ever thought about becoming a priest?"

Lolek chuckled. As he walked home that evening he thought about what the blaster said. He also recalled the question his mother had asked him before she died.

The year Lolek turned nineteen the winter seemed endless. His father had been very ill. Lolek always remembered to bring home soup and medicine after work.

"Papa, I'm home!" he called one evening. But there was no answer. He stared at his father lying in bed. "Papa, are you asleep?" Still no answer.

Lolek placed his shaky palm over his father's hands. Lolek's father had died.

First Mama, then Edmund, and now Papa.

"Goodbye, Papa," he cried.

Never before had Lolek felt so . . .

Alone.

Winter passed and Lolek finally felt like a grown man. People stopped calling him by his childhood name. He was now just Karol to all who met him.

Karol still missed his father, just as he missed Mama and Edmund. But he found joy in acting. During the war, Karol and his friends put on plays in secret. They did this to give the Polish people hope.

Karol had another secret in his heart, too. At first he didn't talk about it. But the secret grew and grew inside him, until he couldn't keep it hidden any more.

"Are you really going to leave the theater to become a priest?" a good friend asked.

Karol answered, "Yes."

"But you could do great things for Poland as an actor," said another.

"You're right," Karol explained, "but God is asking me to be a priest."

Karol's friends were not surprised. His love for God had never been a secret. But they also knew how dangerous it was to become a priest during the war.

Karol and the other young men preparing to be priests were very careful. They knew that if they were caught, it would cost them their lives.

Finally, a few years later, the war ended. Poland was at peace, and the Jews were once again free.

Still, Jerzy was nowhere to be found. Karol couldn't find anyone who knew what had happened to him. Perhaps Jerzy had died fighting in the war. Maybe he had moved far away. Or maybe he had been captured. All Karol knew was that his best friend was gone.

As he finished his studies to become a priest, Karol was filled with joy. But there was one thing he worried about. *When my mother died a little bit of me went with her, Karol thought. And more of me leaves each time I lose someone I love. Edmund, Papa, Jerzy . . . they're all gone. After this war I don't know if I'll have any love left to give God—or anyone else.*

Karol pulled some petals off a flower and let the wind catch them. *Maybe losing the people you love doesn't mean losing everything. Lord,* he prayed, *fill my heart with love.*

Shortly after he became a priest, Karol was
sent to Rome to study even more. The city was
beautiful. There he saw places he had only read
about in books.

In the meantime, another kind of darkness had
come to Poland. The new Communist leaders

threatened both freedom and faith. People weren't allowed to practice their religion. Those who tried to pray or worship openly were punished. Karol made a promise to himself. *Someday,* he thought, *I will go home and help the people remember who loves them most.*

When Karol returned to Poland, he spent most of his time with young people. Together they took many trips to the mountains so they could talk freely about God.

"Father, what should we call you so people won't know you are a priest?"

"Call me 'Uncle,'" he laughed.

The mountains and rivers were a perfect playground. They could kayak, hike, play games—and pray. It was also a great place to ask for advice.

"Fath—I mean—Uncle?" one of the young women said.

"Yes?" he answered, looking up from his book.

"A young man has asked me to marry him, and I haven't said yes yet." She tugged at her braid nervously.

"Do you *want* to say yes?"

"I think so, but do *you* think it's a good idea?"

"I'll ask you something my mother once asked me," Karol said. "Who do you love most?"

She hesitated, then smiled.

"If you're sure of your answer, then I'm sure it's a good idea." Then he playfully added. "But are you sure you want to marry *him*?"

They both laughed as she got up and ran to the young man with her answer.

As the sky grew dim, they all gathered for Mass. Father Karol raised his eyes and remembered all those he loved: his mother, father, brother, friends— everyone who had once roamed the same mountains with him and who never would again. In that moment he knew. The gift of Jesus he held between his fingertips was not meant to stay hidden high in the peaceful peaks. It was time to share God's love openly in the cities below.

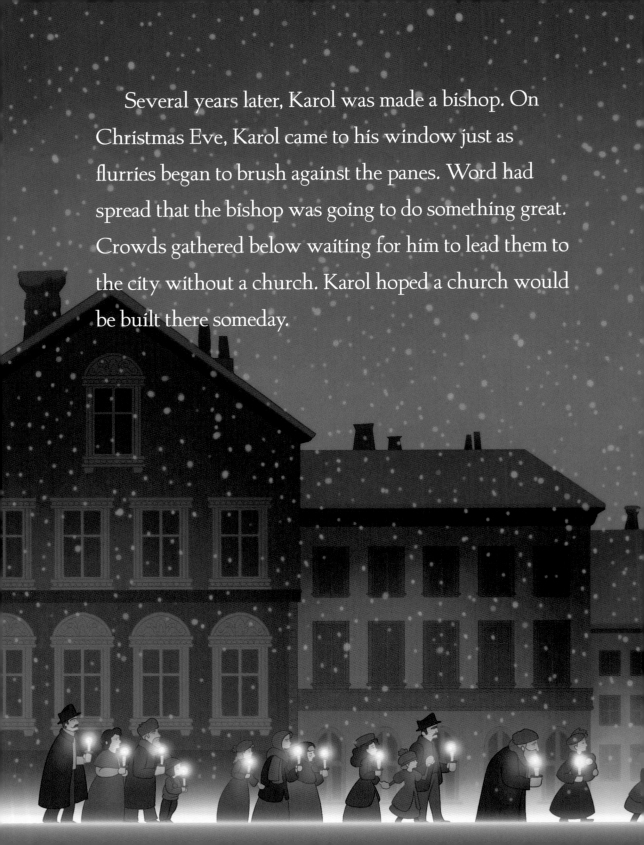

Several years later, Karol was made a bishop. On Christmas Eve, Karol came to his window just as flurries began to brush against the panes. Word had spread that the bishop was going to do something great. Crowds gathered below waiting for him to lead them to the city without a church. Karol hoped a church would be built there someday.

He stepped into the night with a glowing candle.
They all began to walk. Tanks and soldiers lined the
way. They too had heard that something was going to
happen. They had orders to stop Bishop Karol and the
people. But the crowd overflowed; there were too many
to take captive.

Finally, they arrived at a large field where hundreds more had gathered. The army waited and watched as a giant cross made by the metal workers was planted deep into the ground. Underneath it stood Karol. His voice echoed in the night air:

"The people of this city belong to God. And the children of God want a church!" he said.

Midnight struck, and Karol courageously delivered the Christmas present he had wanted so long to give: a Mass for all to see.

The army watched. The people listened on their knees. And Karol gave thanks for this great moment.

It wasn't long before Karol became an archbishop.
He traveled to Rome often and took walks through
the city when he could. One day, Archbishop Karol
noticed that a man about his age was staring at him.
The man was holding a newspaper. He kept looking at
it, then at him. Karol walked toward the man. His face
seemed familiar. His eyes were just like . . .

"Jerzy? Is it really you?"

"Lolek!"

Karol ran to his friend and hugged him. It had been a long time since anybody had called him Lolek.

"Where have you been?" Karol asked.

"Everywhere—except Poland. Everything I loved there is gone. How are you doing, Lolek?"

"I'm well. I've been here a month, but I miss Poland."

"I read in this newspaper that you've been doing great things, just like I said you would. It says here that you even got the government's permission to build a new church. Keep that up and they'll make you pope!"

Karol sighed, "There's so much left to do in Poland. The Communists still control everything. But the peoples' faith is growing stronger."

The two friends met often until it was time for Karol to leave Rome.

The Polish people were happy to see him again. Archbishop Karol had become a cardinal of the Church. This meant that now Cardinal Karol would help choose a new pope when one was needed.

One August he traveled to Rome to join the other cardinals from around the world. They gathered to choose a new Holy Father. When the votes were counted, a smiling Italian cardinal was elected—Pope John Paul I.

Karol returned home. One month later, however, he received some unexpected news. Pope John Paul I had died suddenly. All the cardinals were called back to Rome.

This time, Karol wondered. *They would never choose me, would they? Of course not!* he thought. *There are a hundred reasons to elect someone else. Besides, there has never been a pope from Poland.*

Karol asked God to help him. *Surely, Lord, you have a plan,* he prayed. *And I know who I love most.*

Trusting in God, Karol left for Rome. He had shown the Polish people how to keep their hearts free. He prayed that would be enough.

The cardinals walked across Saint Peter's Square to the Sistine Chapel. When all the cardinals were inside, the door was locked with a key. The election began. The next few days of voting would be long.

As the votes were counted, Karol heard his name called. Then he heard it again. Everyone heard it. It was impossible *not* to hear it. Louder and faster his name was spoken. And then, "Cardinal Karol from Poland, we have chosen you to be our pope. Do you accept?"

Karol trembled. He would have to answer.

Karol's mind flooded with memories. Suddenly, he heard another voice speaking gently in his heart.

"Lolek, do *you* love me?"

"You know I do, Jesus."

"Lolek, do you *love* me?"

"You know that I love you, Lord," he answered again.

"But, Lolek, who do you love *most*?"

"I love you, Jesus. I love you the most."

"Then take care of the ones I love."

"Always."

The chapel was silent. The cardinals waited for his answer. Cardinal Karol's voice was strong, "Yes, I accept!"

He had said goodbye to his mother, his brother, and his father, goodbye to his friends and his homeland, too. There, with a full heart, he even said goodbye to his name and took a new one— Pope John Paul II. Remembering who he loved most, the new pope realized that he hadn't lost anything at all.

His white robes rustled in the wind as he stepped onto the balcony. A sea of beaming faces greeted him below. *What will this pope from a faraway land be like?* they wondered. *Will he love us?* The moment they saw him, they knew he did.

For the rest of his life, Pope John Paul II never forgot he loved God most of all. He shared that love with the whole world. And everywhere he went, crowds came out to greet him, shouting, "John Paul Two, we love you!"

Fabiola Garza is an illustrator and concept artist based in New England. She attended Rhode Island School of Design, and her clients include Hasbro, HitPoint Studios, and Callaway Digital Arts. Saint John Paul II is a major source of inspiration and consolation in Fabiola's life. *The Story of Saint John Paul II: A Boy Who Became Pope* is her first book for children. Fabiola hopes to inspire the young and the young at heart alike to reach new heights of both holiness and whimsy with the pictures and words she creates. Her gallery and projects can be found at www.fabiolagarza.com.

Who are the Daughters of St. Paul?

We are Catholic sisters. Our mission is to be like Saint Paul and tell everyone about Jesus! There are so many ways for people to communicate with each other. We want to use all of them so everyone will know how much God loves us. We do this by printing books (you're holding one!), making radio shows, singing, helping people at our bookstores, using the Internet, and in many other ways.

Visit our Web site at www.pauline.org

Library of Congress Cataloging-in-Publication Data

Garza, Fabiola.
The story of Saint John Paul II : a boy who became pope / written and illustrated by Fabiola Garza.
pages cm
ISBN-13: 978-0-8198-9013-9
ISBN-10: 0-8198-9013-8
1. John Paul II, Pope, 1920-2005--Juvenile literature. I. Title.
BX1378.5.G3785 2013
282.092--dc23
[B]

2013033503

Illustrated by Fabiola Garza

"P" and PAULINE are registered trademarks of the Daughters of Saint Paul.

Published by Pauline Books & Media, 50 Saint Pauls Avenue, Boston, MA 02130-3491

Printed in the U.S.A.

SSJP VSAUSAPEOILL9-23J13-10004 9013-8

www.pauline.org

Pauline Books & Media is the publishing house of the Daughters of Saint Paul, an international congregation of women religious serving the Church with the communications media.

1 2 3 4 5 6 7 8 9   18 17 16 15 14